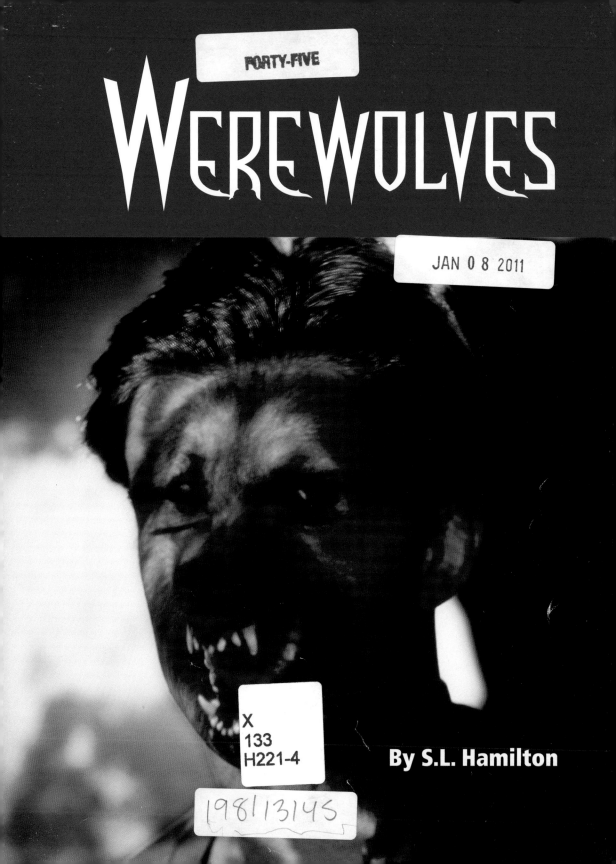

Visit us at
www.abdopublishing.com

Published by ABDO Publishing Company, 8000 West 78th Street, Suite 310, Edina, MN 55439. Copyright ©2011 by Abdo Consulting Group, Inc. International copyrights reserved in all countries. No part of this book may be reproduced in any form without written permission from the publisher. A&D Xtreme™ is a trademark and logo of ABDO Publishing Company.

Printed in the United States of America, North Mankato, Minnesota.
052010
092010

Editor: John Hamilton
Graphic Design: Sue Hamilton
Cover Design: John Hamilton
Cover Photo: Corbis
Interior Photos: ASC Games-pg 28; Bethesda Softworks-pg 29; Corbis-pgs 12, 13, 23, 24, & 25; Getty Images-pgs 14 & 15; Granger Collection-pgs 10 & 11; iStockphoto-pgs 2, 3, 4, 5, 7, 16, 17, 18, & 19; Mary Evans Picture Library-pgs 20 & 21; North Wind Picture Archives-pgs 8 & 9; Photo Researchers-pg 1; Screen Media Ventures-pg 26; Sega-pg 29; Sony Pictures-pg 27; Summit Entertainment-pg 26; Thinkstock-pgs 6, 30 & 31; Universal Pictures-pgs 24 & 26; Warner Bros-pg 25.

Library of Congress Cataloging-in-Publication Data

Hamilton, Sue L., 1959-
  Werewolves / S.L. Hamilton.
    p. cm. -- (Xtreme monsters)
  Includes index.
  ISBN 978-1-61613-471-6
  1. Werewolves--Juvenile literature. I. Title.
  GR830.W4H36 2011
  398'.469--dc22

                              2010002744

CONTENTS

XTREME

Werewolves are shape-shifters. When the moon is full, these monsters change from human to wolf and back again. For centuries, they have terrorized people around the world. Werewolves cannot control their beastly actions, often killing anyone who gets in their way.

WEREWOLVES

Xtreme Quote

"All of us are God's creatures, but some are more creature than others."

WEREWOLF

The first werewolf story came from ancient Greece. The myth said that Arcadia's King Lykaon invited Zeus to dinner. To test the god's holiness, Lykaon served him a slaughtered child, waiting to see if Zeus would eat. The king of the gods was furious and turned Lykaon into a wolf.

Xtreme Definition

Lycanthrope /noun/ From the Greek *lukanthropos* meaning "wolf man."

HISTORY

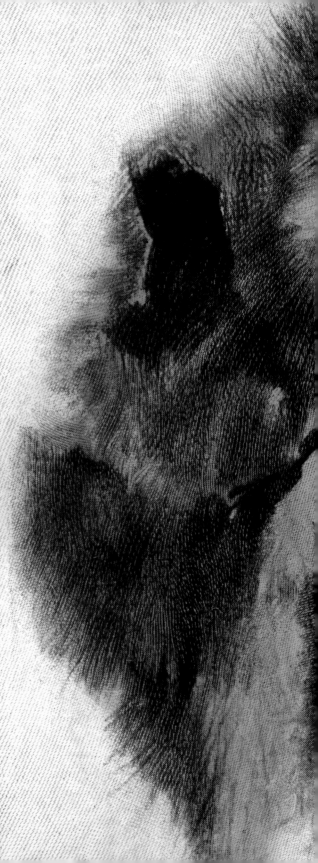

Loup-Garou

For hundreds of years, Europeans believed werewolves roamed their forests. In 1764, a giant wolf attacked people in an area of France called Gévaudan. The Beast of Gévaudan killed several people. Hunters shot at the beast, but it escaped and was back killing days later. Some believed the animal had supernatural powers. It was called loup-garou: werewolf.

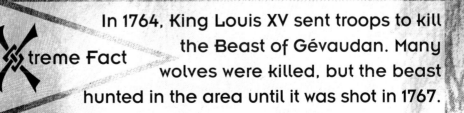

In 1764, King Louis XV sent troops to kill the Beast of Gévaudan. Many wolves were killed, but the beast hunted in the area until it was shot in 1767.

Xtreme Fact

Werewolf Trials

In the past, several people were convicted of being werewolves. A famous case was the 1590 trial of Peter Stump near Cologne, Germany. A serial killer, Stump convinced officials that he was given a belt by a demon that allowed him to turn into a werewolf. Stump was tried and found guilty. Given the death sentence, he was tortured and beheaded.

Xtreme Fact

Some people were accused of being werewolves because they wore wolf skins for warmth. It was thought people took on the animals' powers.

BECOMING A

Legend says that the way to become a werewolf is to be bitten or scratched by another werewolf. A curse may also cause an unfortunate victim to become a werewolf at the next full moon.

Xtreme Quote

"Even a man who is pure in heart and says his prayers by night may become a wolf when the wolfsbane blooms and the autumn moon is bright." ~The Wolf Man

WEREWOLF

Werewolfism in Families

Some believe that werewolfism is passed down from father to son. The lycanthrope powers may lay dormant until needed, or may become active as a child enters adulthood.

Xtreme Definition

Yennork /noun/ A person from a werewolf family who cannot shape-shift into a werewolf.

STRENGTHS AND

A werewolf is said to have the enhanced powers of a wolf. Like a wolf, a werewolf has superior night vision and a good sense of smell. Plus, a werewolf is strong, fast, cunning, and able to heal quickly when wounded.

X̽treme Quote

"I could not care less if I am a 'freak.' I don't care what other people think about me. I am me." ~Anonymous Werewolf

Weaknesses

Weaknesses

It's said that pure silver can kill werewolves. A silver bullet, knife, or spear may be used to end a werewolf's life. Quicksilver, a toxic liquid metal, may also destroy a werewolf. Violent blows to the head and heart stops the powerful creature, but its head or heart must be cut away to really kill a werewolf.

REAL-LIFE

WEREWOLVES

A medical condition known as clinical lycanthropy is a rare disorder that makes a person believe he or she can turn into animals, such as wolves.

Werewolf Syndrome

Hypertrichosis, or werewolf syndrome, is a rare disease that causes excessive hair growth all over a person's body. Carnival sideshow acts such as Alice the Minnesota Woolly Child, Jo-Jo the Dog-Face Boy, and Lionel the Lion-Faced Man were people with hypertrichosis.

Alice

Jo-Jo

Lionel

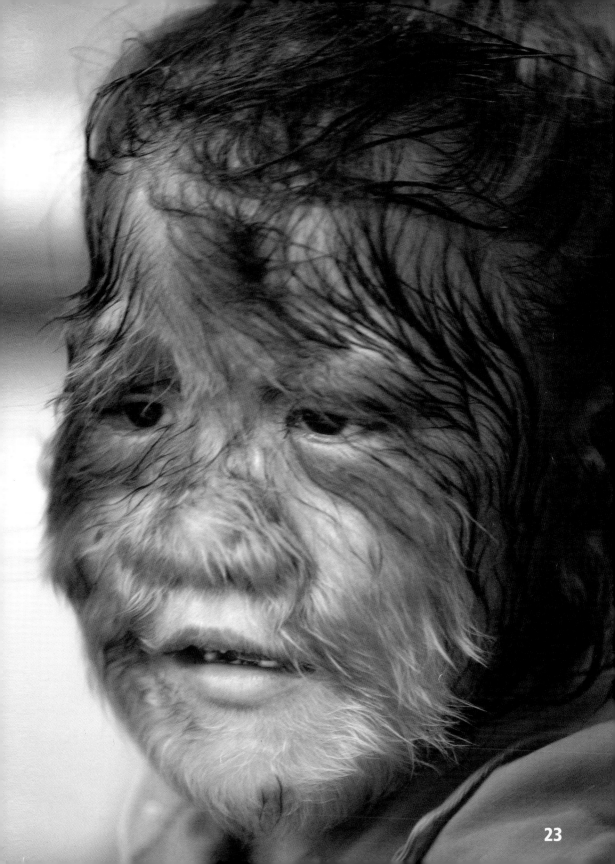

WEREWOLF

Werewolves have been in films since the mid-1930s.

Universal Pictures' 1935 film *Werewolf of London* was the first werewolf movie produced by a major studio.

The most famous werewolf film was 1941's *The Wolf Man,* starring Lon Chaney Jr.

MOVIES

The 1981 film *An American Werewolf in London* combined comedy and horror in a tale of an unlucky tourist.

A brother's secret becomes his sister's nightmare in the 1996 film *Bad Moon*.

Werewolf Movies

In 2010, Universal Pictures released *The Wolfman*, a remake of the 1941 classic about a cursed family.

THE WOLFMAN

The *Twilight* saga is based on the best-selling books by Stephenie Meyer. It tells the story of human Bella Swan, vampire Edward Cullen, and werewolf Jacob Black.

the twilight saga
new moon

in the 21st Century

In the 2009 film *Underworld: Rise of the Lycans*, a feud arises between vampire Death Dealers and werewolf Lycans.

In 2002's *Dog Soldiers*, a training mission goes bad when soldiers seek shelter in a farmhouse overrun with werewolves.

WEREWOLF

Werewolves are the subject of several adventure games. Sometimes the werewolf is an evil character to be hunted and destroyed, while other games make the werewolf a hero.

WEREWOLF
THE APOCALYPSE

GAMES

BLOODMOON

ALTERED BEAST

THE

Arcadia
Also spelled Arkadia. A region of southern Greece.

Curse
When a practitioner of magic wishes evil or misfortune to happen to another person. It was thought that gypsies could curse individuals or families, forcing them to become werewolves.

Legend
A story about supernatural people, beings, or events told throughout the ages. Although a legend may be made up, many people believe it to be true.

Louis XV
The king of France from 1715 to 1774.

Lycanthrope
The Greek word for werewolf, or a person who can change from human to wolf and back again.

GLOSSARY

Quicksilver
Another name for mercury, a toxic, silver-colored metal. It is used in thermometers to measure temperature.

Serial Killer
A person who kills three or more people in a short period of time.

Shape-Shift
To change in physical appearance. Werewolves are people who can shape-shift into wolves.

Wolfsbane
A type of poisonous plant. Wolfsbane was given its name when it was used to kill wolves in attempts to rid them from an area. The plant was added to meat that was used as bait.

Zeus
In Greek mythology, the supreme king of the gods.

INDEX